The School of War

Alexandre Najjar

The School of War

Translated from the French by
Laurie Wilson

TELEGRAM

ISBN 10: 1-84659-009-4
ISBN 13: 978-1-84659-009-2

First published as *L'école de la guerre*
by Editions Balland, Paris, 1999

This edition published 2006 by Telegram Books

A full CIP record for this book is available from the British Library
A full CIP record for this book is available from the Library of Congress

Manufactured in Lebanon by Chemaly & Chemaly

TELEGRAM
26 Westbourne Grove
London W2 5RH
www.telegrambooks.com

To the memory of Robert Najjar

Contents

Prologue

All wars are alike. What I experienced in Lebanon, others experienced in France, in Spain, in Yugoslavia or elsewhere. Yes, all wars are alike, because while weapons change, the men who wage and are subjected to war do not in the least. As a child, I sometimes heard my Uncle Michel talk about 'Big Bertha'. I thought he was talking about an aunt or a distant cousin. It was not until later – much later – that I understood that he had appropriated the nickname given to an enormous German howitzer during the Great War, so he could talk about the war without frightening us. 'Big Bertha' ... Eighty years later, on the brink of the third millennium, in a country located on the shores of the Mediterranean, the same code-name, the same ugly war, the same tragedy.

When I resolved to return to Lebanon, after a seven-year absence, I was seized by a double sense of anxiety: that of seeing the past catch up with me, and that of being disappointed by the postwar situation. I had left the Country of Cedars after fifteen years of having, with all my strength, resisted a violence that spared nothing. I had *frequented* the war like one frequents a lady of the night, had drained my cup to the last dregs. Once peace had been re-established, I had decided to go elsewhere for a breath of fresh air, as if, my mission accomplished, I suddenly felt the need to clear my mind, to forget the drama I had endured, under another sky.

The war was an unbearable nightmare for me, but was also – how could I deny it? – an excellent schooling in life's lessons. Hemingway said that 'any war experience is priceless for a writer.' I would like to believe that. Without the war, I would have been another man. All my life, I will undoubtedly regret not having had a peaceful childhood (I was eight when the war broke out, twenty-three when the guns were silenced) and having often seen death from too short a distance. But these regrets, these trials, have given me a new understanding of happiness. A day without bombings, a bridge that isn't under sniper siege, a night without a blackout, a road without barricades, a clear sky across which no rockets shoot ... for me, all of this will henceforth be synonymous with happiness.

As for 'Bertha', now that I know the truth, I prefer to believe, as I did as a child, that she is a plump old lady who strolls through the streets in her big white hat, smiling at children and handing out candy to them.

Beirut, June 1999

Esthetics of the Shell

'*Ahlan wa sahlan!*'

Aunt Malaké greets me, and I give her a kiss and enter the living room, walking into a heavy aroma of tobacco and honey.

'You still smoke your *narghile*?'

'It's my favorite pastime,' she replies, shrugging her shoulders.

Nothing has changed in this house: the slightly outdated furniture, the painting of the opera singer Umm Kulthum, the black-and-white portrait of Uncle Jamil, and the cat hair on the blue carpet. On a coffee table, near the buffet, a bouquet of white roses in a cylindrical container.

'What is that?'

'A shell case. It's decorative, don't you think?'

'Decorative' … This word takes me back fifteen years. The first shell, like a baptism.

The first shell was lying at the base of a 240mm gun mounted in a schoolyard in Achrafieh. Around the gun stood three permanently assigned militiamen who, on a day of truce, invited me to share their snack. Until then, I had thought shells were invisible – I saw them explode far off in the distance in a geyser of smoke, encircle the bombed villages with an ephemeral halo, set houses and pine forests ablaze; I heard their din as they crashed down on my neighbourhood, or their whistle as they sliced through the air over the house … To *see* a shell, to caress it, was a revelation for me. With its oblong, esthetically faultless form, its generous curves, its nose cone that recalls the contours of a breast, its elegant blue-grey colour, and the brilliance of its steel casing, polished like a piece of marble, a shell is beautiful, marked by perfect beauty. To the touch, it is cold and hard; who would believe it could explode into a thousand pieces? Oddly, it emits a sense of security. So who dreamed up this instrument that combines obesity and beauty so well? Was it to highlight the precariousness of all things beautiful or out of perfectionism that its creator took such care to polish this projectile that in the end disintegrates as it disseminates terror? I deduced that this unknown artist, along with the sniper, was among those who lend their art to the service of Death and who seek perfection in murder itself.

The second time I saw a shell I felt a sense of fear that I had not experienced the first time. During the night a shell had crashed to the ground only a few yards from where I lived. Miraculously, it had landed in the road without exploding. At daybreak, the local baker noticed it and called the entire neighbourhood out into the street.

'*Azifé ya chabéb! Azifé ma nfajarét!*'

I was awoken by his cries: 'A shell, everyone, an unexploded shell!' and I very naturally went down into the street to witness the event. At a safe distance from the object, a circle of curious onlookers had formed. I joined in. The projectile had bored into the asphalt, like a javelin in the sand, leaving only its base exposed for us to see.

'If it had exploded, it wouldn't have left a single house standing,' the baker exclaimed.

'Not so loud,' his neighbour murmured, elbowing him. 'You might revive it.'

'It looks like a suppository,' one of the kids observed.

'The priest ran towards us, a censer in hand.

'It's divine providence.'

'It's divine providence,' the crowd echoed.

He pulled a picture of Our Lady of Perpetual Help out of the pocket of his cassock. He carefully approached the projectile, set his picture on the ground, and hurriedly retraced his steps. Next, a housewife moved forward, brandishing a bouquet of daisies. She decorated the area with flowers and backed up to her place in the circle.

'Let us pray,' the priest proposed.

The members of the congregation crossed themselves, then said a prayer:

> *Remember, O Virgin Mother of God, when you stand in the sight of the Lord, to speak good things on our behalf, that He may turn away His anger from us.*

The ceremony would have continued had it not been for the arrival of the warrant officer, who was greeted with applause. The warrant officer was the army's official mine clearance expert. In great demand, he responded to the requests of all belligerents – regardless of their loyalties or convictions – with the selflessness of a country doctor. I had previously only seen him in television reports recounting his exploits, and I must confess I had prayed to the Almighty that I would never have occasion to see him in person.

Having arrived within a step or two of the projectile, the warrant officer raised his hand in a call for silence. And the crowd fell silent. He circled the shell four or five times, then went down on one knee, opened a small case, and took out his gear.

'Move thirty yards back,' he ordered.

The crowd moved away, backing up as if they were a single body.

Hidden behind a utility pole, I couldn't follow the progression of his operation. While his hands fiddled with the shell, I couldn't help but think of the temerity of this being who flirted with Death on a daily basis. How did he bring himself to handle this device that could very well blow up in his face? What did he have in the place of a heart that kept him from fearing that one unsteady movement of his fingers could make everything blow?

The warrant officer finally stood back up. He wiped his hands in the midst of a cathedral-like silence. He gathered his things, bowed his head to the picture of the Virgin set next to the shell, then, with a satisfied sigh, said:

'It's over.'

He was showered with cheers. The women came out on their balconies and tossed rice, while the curious moved closer to touch him. The neighbourhood's inhabitants forgot everything – war, deaths, shortages – to acclaim the hero. As he passed near me, an older woman drew him to her breast and placed a loud kiss on his forehead.

'We all admire your courage,' she cried enthusiastically.

The warrant officer did not blush. He wiped his brow and replied, unshaken:

'What you call *courage*, Ma'am, I call *knowledge*.'

Fireworks

In the living room of my family home, I contemplate my sleeping mother. She has aged a little. But the gentleness has not left her face, which is lit up by a satisfied smile. I can sense that she is happy I have returned. I observe her hands – they are the hands of a tired woman, worn by time and by the war.

When I replay the scenes of my childhood, the image of my mother, standing or moving through a swarm of kids, is ever-present. I am the second of five children, which perhaps explains why at no point during my childhood did I ever experience boredom. Moreover, boredom was a notion that was totally unknown to me. One of my friends, who was an only child, would endlessly complain about what he called *al dajar*: boredom. I was so tormented by this word, whose meaning I was not familiar with, that I asked my mother about it. She had a terrible time describing the feeling of emptiness and melancholy, undoubtedly because she herself had forgotten all about boredom in the midst of our tribe.

My memories of my pre-war childhood are sparse, and above all cushioned in a feeling of lightheartedness, a true godsend that is lost as we grow up. Then came the war. Without warning, it interrupted the daily existence of an entire people, requiring them to adapt to a new situation, to radically change their way of life, to set aside their joys and pleasures. We children were far from realizing the true extent of the danger or that the enemy militia were bearing down on our city – it wasn't that we were too foolish to follow the progression of the operations, but we were naive enough to believe the adults' stories.

'It's nothing, children. Just fireworks.'

This single sentence – my mother's innovation – had been enough to transform the din of shells exploding above our house into a carnival. The first time a shell fell near where we lived, in the middle of the night, I was terrified. It was like a violent storm: a flash, a light zig-zagging across the sky, a rumble, and the shaking of the windows. I pulled the covers up over my head.

'It's nothing, sweetheart. It's only fireworks.'

My mother's soothing voice, her warm hand on my forehead, and this lie that, though it was derisory, worked wonders. Our fear gave way to joy, the very kind we would feel on September 1 – Saint Simon the Stylite's Day – when the vendors would set up their booths and sell candy, and musicians would lead the *dabké* and other popular dances. The earth could stop turning – the idea that a carnival, fireworks and all, was in full swing only a few blocks from where we lived made us the happiest kids in the world.

A Lebanese proverb says that 'a lie is on a short rope'. I learned the truth thanks to a cousin who was less credulous than I was. I felt a deep sense of disappointment – so all of those celebrations *hadn't* taken place – as if I had been had and, above all, I felt a *retroactive* fright, stirred up by the awareness of my casual attitude towards shells.

'Why did you hide the truth from me?' I asked my mother.

'I didn't want to traumatize all of you ...'

'So you lied to us.'

'It was a "white lie". I twisted reality to delude your fear.'

'To delude fear' ... How could I be angry at my mother, with that disarming smile of hers.

'I don't regret having lied to you, not for a minute. The enemy was only a hundred yards away and your faces were radiant. Without the optimism I read in your eyes, I couldn't have made it through.'

Today, as I watch my mother sleeping, I bless the innocence that led us to believe all that she told us, and without which shells never would have been fireworks.

Snipers

The bridge had been dubbed the 'ring', though no one really knew why. Perhaps because during the war years it had been the scene of extremely violent fighting. It connected the eastern Christian side of Beirut to the western Muslim side of the capital. From the balcony of my family home I observe it, squinting. The morning wind tousles my hair.

'Faster, Moussa, faster!'

The taxi driver's voice resonates in my memory. Only yesterday a myriad of snipers kept watch over the 'ring', their only purpose being to prevent any vehicles from crossing it. Is there anything more cowardly than a sniper? And how did they get their name in the first place? I can only find one explanation that makes any sense: they are called '*francs-tireurs*' (snipers) because they proceed '*franchement*' (straight ahead), without discussion, without a second thought, without the torment of scruples. They act as if they were at a carnival, trying to win the stuffed-bear prizes. They play hide-and-seek with their prey. They take aim – at a child, a woman, a dog – and as soon as the target is in their line of fire, they mechanically pull the trigger. The shoulder supporting the rifle is jolted, the elbow pulls back. The target collapses, moaning or yelping, depending.

I feel a chill run down my spine. Where are those snipers today? Where are they hiding? Maybe they have become ordinary men, decent people, good family men like you run into at the supermarket, on the way out of the mosque on Fridays or at ten o'clock mass on Sundays. Are they nostalgic for the time when they could quench their thirst to kill without anyone or anything bothering them? Do they no longer have itchy trigger fingers?

'Faster, Moussa, faster!'

From out of the past, I hear the voice of the taxi

driver giving himself words of encouragement. I see myself again, sitting next to him in the front seat. Before us lies the 'ring', the bridge of death, that snakes endlessly along in front of the leprous buildings …

Every Saturday Moussa would take me to see Ghada, who lived on the other side of the demarcation line. He drove an ageless car, a white Plymouth with chrome fenders, as big as an aircraft carrier. This vehicle was a second home for him, as it were – he had carefully furnished it and took loving care of the accessories that adorned it. From the rear-view mirror hung a small chain with a blue stone that apparently had the power to avert the Evil Eye. The dashboard was covered with a sort of sheepskin carpet, the colour of which had turned from white to yellow over time. Near the glove compartment, there was a gold plaque that read: *La tétakhar ya baba, nahnou bintizarak*, which means: 'Hurry home Dad, we're waiting for you.'

On the outside, near the exhaust pipe, he had suspended a little baby shoe that, according to Moussa, had belonged to his first child, Rachid. 'It's a good luck charm,' he assured me in a solemn voice. 'Children's shoes ward off evil.'

'Faster, Moussa, faster!'

Moussa straightens up in his seat, grabs the bottle of Johnnie Walker lying next to him, tosses back a shot of whiskey, wipes his mouth with the back of his hand then, clenching his teeth, steps on the accelerator. The Plymouth sets off, its tyres screeching. Thoughts run through my head: it takes about twelve seconds to cross the bridge at sixty miles an hour. They might be the last twelve seconds of my life. My heart jumps. His head tucked down between his shoulders, Moussa drives toward the other end of the bridge at breakneck speed, not knowing whether death or life will greet us upon arrival. He speeds on. Without a second thought. Like the sniper who takes aim at us.

Through the half-open window, the wind blows into the car, whipping my face, whistling in my ears, tousling my hair. If I can feel it, that means I'm still alive. I crouch down in my seat and close my eyes. A shot rings out. One of the back side windows shatters. The wind rushes into the car and sends the glass fragments flying. 'If I can feel it, that means I'm still alive.' I count: 'Eight, seven, six seconds until deliverance' … Second shot. A sharp crack tells me that the bullet has lodged in the body of the car.

'*Asrah, asrah!*'

The pedal to the floor, Moussa curses his car and exhorts it to go faster, as a jockey whips his mount nearing the finish line. Spurred on by the impact of the projectile, the Plymouth takes off. The wind engulfs my face. 'If I can feel it, that means I'm still alive.' A third shot. But it is too late.

I open my eyes. A barricade topped by a red flag – we have arrived. Moussa brakes abruptly. He leans his forehead against the steering wheel and lets out a deep sigh. I relax my jaw.

There is no more wind, but I am alive.

'*Al hamdoulillah aala salama!*'

Moussa pronounces the ritual formula: 'Thank Allah that we made it safe and sound.'

'*Khalas?*'

I ask him if it is over. He replies with a nod. Yes, it's over. I am still among the living.

I open my wallet and pull out a five hundred pound bill. Moussa raises one eyebrow and looks at me mockingly. He motions towards the broken back window with his chin.

'And who's going to pay for the window?'

I hand him two more bills, which he shoves into the pocket of his sweat-soaked shirt. I step out onto the ground and walk around the taxi to assess the damage. A bullet is embedded just inches from the gas tank.

'It's divine providence,' I say.

'No,' Moussa replies, pointing to the little white shoe swinging next to the exhaust pipe. 'It's Rachid's shoe.'

The Barber

'It's been a long time.'

'I've been in Europe ...'

'Ah, Europe!'

Here we go again ... The barber is the same as ever. His boisterousness used to exasperate me. Today I find it comforting – it reassures me that time hasn't really changed the men in this country. During the war, at the first light of dawn, even before the newspaper seller began his day, the old men in the neighbourhood would gather in the barber shop to get the latest news from the front. The barber turns his back to them.

Facing the big mirror that reflects his image, with that of his audience sitting on straw-bottomed stools in the background, he sets to work. He ties the pink smock he has draped over me around my neck, runs his expert fingers through my hair, rotates my chair – a spacious chair with leather arms, perched on a rotating pedestal – and tilts it back towards the sink. I end up with my head in the water and my feet in the air. I close my eyes. With one hand, the barber pours the shampoo onto my scalp – ah, that apple-scented shampoo, still the same as the day my father made me climb up onto this promontory for my first haircut. With the other hand, he rubs my hair. The smooth lather builds up as the water runs. 'Is the temperature OK?' he asks. 'Yes, it's just fine,' I say softly, wiping away the liquid that drips down my temples. He rinses my hair thoroughly, towels it dry vigorously, tilts the chair upright, spins it back around, takes the pair of scissors his apprentice hands to him, then starts to trim the stubborn strands that lie across my forehead. I open my eyes.

'*Chou fi ma fi?*'

The sacramental words have been spoken. Behind me, someone has just asked the usual question: 'What's new?' The barber nods his head with a knowing look. Here we go again ... Without turning towards the others, whose reactions are displayed in the mirror, he paints a panorama of the political and military situation, evaluates the morale of the troops, lists the casualties from the day before, reports the warlords' latest confidences ... Before an audience that he has already won over, he proposes his analysis of the events. Where does he get his information? Is it the figment of an active imagination? Is it trustworthy? My eyelids grow heavy; soothed by the 'snip-snip' of the scissors, I let myself go ... 'I don't think it would be premature to envision a truce in the near future ...' Each of his sentences is carefully weighed: they apprise without committing their speaker, and inform without compromising him. 'France may very well intervene. But ever since de Gaulle left France isn't what it used to be.' Sometimes his tone changes, becomes more assertive: 'You'll see, the war will go on for a hundred years.' The barber knows what he is doing – just as his customer's muscles begin to relax, he *overdoes it*. The result is guaranteed: the customer jumps, begins to worry, opens his eyes wide. 'A hundred years? You really think so?' The scissors move around his ear, shave close to his neck … The barber elaborates. Words come out of his mouth in sync with the falling hair that the apprentice sweeps up into his dustpan.

Loving

Newspapers, books and other assorted objects are piled high in the attic. Stepping into this mouldy odour, I have descended into my past. I used to like to play in this place that was miraculously left untouched by the shells that hit my family home. I look around me: toys, photo albums, a stroller, a table-football game, two bicycles … My entire childhood is here, enclosed in this space. On a shelf, next to a string of onions, I see a small studded case. I wipe off the film of dust that has collected on it and cautiously lift the lid. They are still here. Dozens of letters, each folded in four, carefully arranged, love letters that Ghada used to send to me. I would read them in secret ... Between her house and mine, the 'ring', the bridge of disunion. When the fighting would escalate and no one dared travel back and forth, I would sulk – how were we to overcome this absence when shells rendered all communication between the two parts of the capital impossible? The telephone? I spent hours dialing her number, in vain.

One morning a friend who worked for the Red Cross offered to put me in contact with her.

'Write to her – I'll deliver it.'

'How will you manage to get to the other side?'

'Until further notice, they aren't firing at ambulances.' he replied with a wink.

From then on I started writing torrid love letters, melancholy and full of hope. Ghada replied. In black ink, on blue paper, she wrote passionate letters that I kept like jewels in this case she gave me for my sixteenth birthday ...

I pull out a letter at random and unfold it. It sends a shiver through my body. God, these letters bring back memories:

My love,

I am counting the hours that separate me from peace so I can finally see you again and take you in my arms. I hunger for you, I need your gaze, your smile, your fragrance ...

I hear explosions. The war, still and always. Shells are falling and I don't know if they are falling on you. I wish ... I wish I were an angel, a bird, so I could fly over that bridge of death, that bridge of shame that keeps me from you! I am afraid, my love. Afraid of dying far from you, of leaving this world all alone. Heaven? I don't want it if you aren't there! If we were together, you and I, holding each other close, we would be strong, indestructible. But here, one without the other, we are defenseless, unarmed, vulnerable!

I hear 'launchings'. Yet again, it is the gun from the barracks across the street being unleashed. The shells are going to crash down on your neighbourhood, on your street, on your house, maybe. And here I am, powerless, unable to defend you, on my knees. I pray ... I pray that the gunner miscalculate, that he miss his target, that the shells plunge into the sea without causing any damage ... And I impatiently await the end of this war that drags on.

In your last letter, you wrote that you were suffocating, that you couldn't take it any longer. You must be strong, my love. You must resist. We too are resistance fighters, in our own way. If the war is the enemy of love, then we will be the Resistance fighters of love!

It will not defeat us.

Under Fire

Byblos. Sitting by the sea, I breathe in deeply. The sun, the sand, the palm trees, the girls in bikinis, the fragrance of the sea and suntan oil …

An explosion jolts me out of my reverie. Everyone panics.

'What's going on? Was that a shell?'

The lifeguard – bronzed skin, chest thrust out, muscles flexed – circulates among the sunbathers, reassuring them:

'It's nothing, it's for a movie. The military pyrotechnicians forewarned us.'

'A movie?'

'A movie about the war, filmed by a Bulgarian.'

'*Yélaan abou!*'

I let the curse slip out. Can't we sunbathe in peace? I look around me. The spell has been broken – the glaring sun is too strong, the sand is strewn with trash, the palm trees are dishevelled, the girls are callipygian, and the air reeks of fried food. I am upset with myself for having lost my touch, for having let my weaponry-recognition skills slip, for not having been able to distinguish between the blast of a mock explosive device and that of a shell. It used to be child's play for me:

'Is that a "launching" or a "landing"?' everyone would ask me.

I would put my finger to my lips to demand silence, furrow my brow to look more important, and cup my hand around my ear.

'It's a "launching" – our guys are bombing.

Or:

'It's a "landing" – we're under fire! Everyone take shelter!'

As the war dragged on, I honed my skills, to the point that before long I could identify the nature of the weapons being used: 'Those are Stalin organs … That's a 240mm gun … That's just a rocket … Those are Grad missiles …' My family admired my capabilities; the youngest kids thought I was some kind of soothsayer.

My information was supplemented by the precious advice of a schoolteacher who, when a truce made it possible for us to go to school, took it upon himself to inculcate us with the *Ten Steps to Better Survival.* He taught us the art of taking shelter, of criss-crossing the window panes with tape to prevent glass shards in case of an explosion, to seek out possible hiding places while walking down the street in case of a surprise attack, to stock up on supplies during shortages … He taught us the 'three methods for building barricades':

1. Classic barricades, built with sandbags. 'The main drawback,' he warned us, 'is that they are messy when it rains.'

2. Barricades made from cinder blocks, carefully aligned along the area to be protected. 'It's solid,' he assured us, 'but rather expensive.'

3. Barricades built out of old tyres, easy to dismantle

but more dangerous than the preceding barricades because there was a risk of their catching fire.

He handed out a pamphlet, the contents of which I learned by heart:

There is no one neighbourhood in Beirut, no one building in a neighbourhood, no one bedroom in a building – not any longer – that is less exposed than the others. The danger is now the same everywhere. Move only if it is to put a greater number of ceilings and floors between yourself and the sky. Thus far, a bomb has never passed through more than three floors. Draw your own conclusion.

A thickness of a few inches of wood or cotton does not offer much resistance to a hundred pounds of steel. This is a word of advice to those who hide under their tables or their beds when they are frightened.

Getting upset will do nothing to protect you from danger. If the nocturnal din keeps you from sleeping, put some cotton in your ears and take a sleeping pill – two precautionary measures are better than one. And if your house collapses, there is still a chance that you will awaken.

I later learned that this advice was taken from a press release that had been published on the front page of a daily French-language Lebanese newspaper at the time of the fighting between the Anglo-Gaullist forces and the Vichy troops in the Middle East. It didn't teach us anything new, but to its credit it raised our survival instinct to the status of precepts.

I was occasionally mistaken, however. One day, while my entire family was leisurely having breakfast, an explosion shook the house:

"Launching" or "landing"?' my mother asked me, jumping to her feet. Caught off-guard, I hazarded a guess:

'It was a launching. Our guys are bombing!'

My mother put her hand over her heart to calm its beating, then sat back down.

Ten seconds later a salvo of shells crashed around our house and, panicking, we rushed down to the basement – a cramped basement, the entrance of which was blocked by a tottering door. Huddled up against one another, sick with fear, we remained shut in there for two hours, our eyes glued to the door that was keeping Death out, but that the least explosion might blow off its hinges.

A cease-fire was finally announced on the radio. Glad to still be alive, we left the basement to assess the damage. My mother grabbed me by the elbow and pulled me aside.

'That wasn't a launching,' she said through clenched teeth.

Home-schooling

Early one morning, seeing the neighbour's son climb onto the bus wearing a cumbersome backpack, I slapped my forehead. School! The smell of new books the first day back, the desks we would carve pictures into, the chalk dust floating in the air, the ringing of the bell that set us free, the playground whose every nook and cranny we knew by heart … I have never entirely left school. Some nights I wake with a start from a dream about the following day's exam; I forget that there are no more exams and that I have made it past that turning point.

During the war, our school was often closed because of bombardments. That meant long vacations, vacations that could go on for six months. Then, thanks to a lull, we would once again be on the school benches. That was quite an ordeal – we had to wean ourselves from idleness, recall how to study, leave behind our card games and our children's games …

More than once the school itself changed location. That made us feel like we were gypsies and our wagon was the school, studying in a different place every day. The school left Beirut for the suburbs; a shell fell onto the playground. It moved further from the capital; the gunner located it and made this fact known. So the desks and chalkboards were hauled to Bickfaya, to a convent lost somewhere in the countryside … The bus drivers in charge of picking up the kids took senseless risks. They drove at breakneck speed to avoid the snipers' bullets and slalomed through the alleyways, fleeing the bombardments …

Confused, parents no longer knew whether they were to follow the school or whether the school should be near where they lived. As a result, a number of kids changed schools like they changed shirts, depending where their parents found refuge. One of my friends had such irregular schooling that he can pride himself on having attended seventeen different schools.

To deal with the situation, my mother resolved to start a school at home. She ordered a chalkboard from the carpenter, bought boxes of chalk and set up round tables in the living room. Teachers would come in the afternoon to teach us Arabic, French, English and maths, and the kids were placed according to their level. Before long, friends and neighbours joined us, to the point that there ended up being as many as fifteen pupils at the 'Home-School'. My mother was in charge of managing things. As 'principal' she took care of setting up the curriculum, verifying that the school ran smoothly, and punishing the problem kids. To make up for the lack of teachers in certain subjects, she taught the history, geography, biology, catechism and physical education classes herself ... I have unforgettable memories of biology class. My mother ordered a lamb's heart and brain from the butcher, and gathered frogs and snails in the yard. Using these as visual aids, she explained how the organs or animals functioned, sometimes getting so carried away that she would dissect them, following the instructions in our science book. One day, the jar in which she was storing the two green frogs that were to be her guinea pigs mysteriously opened, and the entire class spent the afternoon searching for the two fugitives under the couches. As for physical education, it was reduced to the very basics. Without a stadium or a gym, we were limited to doing somersaults in the yard …

What was to be temporary lasted for an entire year. We took and passed the school exam – the real one – and were admitted to the next grade the following year. Once we were back in school, we had the hardest time clearing our minds of recess in the yard, the cookies Aunt Malaké passed around, and the classroom, with the chalkboard perched on the television set and the pieces of white chalk on the end table. The sight of the principal was enough to stir our nostalgia – with his big belly, the thin beard around his jawline and his yellow teeth, he was nothing like my dear mother.

The Bullet

As I pass through the metal detector at Orly airport for flight 128 to Beirut, a red light comes on accompanied by a screeching whistle.

'Empty your pockets, sir,' the security officer orders.

I put the contents of my pockets into a basket in front of him: a set of keys, some business cards, a crumpled Kleenex, three twenty-centime pieces and a Metro ticket.

'Is that everything?'

'Yes.'

'Step through again.'

I do as ordered. The light comes on, the alarm goes off. The security officer frisks me from head to toe and back up again. He feels my pockets and once again asks me to step through the detector. The result is the same.

'Would you happen to be carrying any metal objects?' he asks me, exasperated.

I pull an X-ray out of my hand luggage.

'What's this?'

'The answer to your question.'

The security officer takes the X-ray, turns toward the window, and holds it up to the light. There is a shiny object in the middle of the negative.

'That's funny,' he says, scratching his head, 'it looks like a bullet.'

I am a survivor. I have a bullet lodged in my chest, even with my heart, but on the right side. It is henceforth an integral part of my organism. I can't feel it, but it is indeed present, embedded in my thorax.

How did it get there? It all started on April 13, 1978. The bus that was taking us home from school was stopped in the suburbs of Beirut – at the Galerie Semaan-Chiyah highway – by a group of young people in combat uniforms who were selling their party's newspaper to drivers. I remember the scene clearly:

'Do you want one?' the militiaman asks the bus driver.

'No thank you,' he replies, shaking his head.

'Everyone buys one,' the militiaman replies.

'You aren't actually going to sell your rag to schoolchildren?'

'What? Say that again, you son-of-a-bitch.'

Sitting at the back of the bus, I straighten up in my seat and watch the militiaman raise his index finger, challenging him. Losing patience, the driver speeds away. He drives past the young man who, enraged, opens fire. A shower of projectiles hits the body of the vehicle. A bullet pierces through the seatback of the bench I am sitting on and ends its flight in my thorax. Blood spews from me in the midst of screams. The windshield shatters. I pass out … A few hours pass before I open my eyes again, at the Hôtel-Dieu de France. I am lying on the operating table, beneath a blinding cross-shaped spotlight. A surgeon and two nurses are bustling around me.

'Your son is out of danger, but we weren't able to remove the bullet.'

'Will he live?' my mother asks in a worried voice.

'Yes, he'll live, but with the bullet.'

Twenty years later, the bullet is still there. I have gotten used to the foreign body that resides in my own body. Removing it wouldn't change anything – the war inhabits me in any case.

Water

I observe Abou Georges, the gardener, as he waters the trees: apple trees, pear trees, mulberry trees, fig trees … Protected by his straw hat as wide as a sombrero, he is not in danger of getting burned by the August sun that is making me feel dizzy. He trudges through the mud; water from the rivulets runs through the irrigation canals that criss-cross the orchard. I am mesmerized by its gurgling – it sounds like laughter.

It was during the war that I learned to appreciate the value of water. Waiting in line with an empty can, I came to understand that it is as vital as the blood that runs through our veins. Before the war, I used to waste water recklessly; I did not think it was of any value. I scorned the odourless, colourless liquid and, to be honest, I preferred soda and alcoholic drinks.

One day, at the height of the fighting, the water disappeared from our faucets, and we did not know why.

'There's no more water,' my mother announced.

'No more water?'

I burst out laughing.

'No more water!'

My mother turned on the faucet. There was a humming sound, but no water.

'No more water!'

I panicked. How could I live without water? Most of my daily rituals depended on that one element: water. How was I to drink, shave, wash my hands, brush my teeth, rinse my hair, take a bath or rinse out the toilet bowl? I was angry at myself for having scorned water, for having denied its benefits, having underestimated its virtues, and, for years, having subjugated rather than venerating it.

We organized ourselves as best we could. 'We'll just have to make the most of things,' my mother decreed.

We started by turning to bottled mineral water. We quickly abandoned this excessively costly method, however. Like all of the neighbourhood's inhabitants, we went and stood in line at the spring that was located in the middle of a basin that had been built during the French Mandate. Until then this basin, which adorned one of the city's main squares, had been no more than a decorative monument like any other. During the shortage it was stormed by a thirsty population. We would wait for an hour or two under the blazing sun to be able to step over the basin's coping and wade through the water, our trouser legs rolled up, to fill our blue jerrycans … To prevent riots, a militiaman kept watch over the line, making sure everyone remained orderly – only his comrades-in-arms were allowed to go against the established procedure – and forbidding any one person from filling more than two cans at a time. 'Make way for the next person,' he barked over and over. The first time, my mother vehemently protested:

'I have five children to bathe.'

'And I have twelve,' someone from the crowd retorted.

She didn't insist. But the following day she found a solution: she handed two blue jerrycans to each of my siblings. For three weeks, the entire family went and stood in line at the spring every morning. Each of us filled two cans and carried them back to the house; Uncle Michel took over from there and emptied the water into the big reservoir on the roof. Water flowed from the faucets once again. But we changed our ways: we learned to *conserve* water.

One day, at last, a neighbourhood shopkeeper bought a tank truck and began to provide households with a fresh supply of water that he collected at the foot of the mountains after the snow thawed. The situation improved.

What has stayed with me from this period? The memory of heated arguments in the long lines, of blue jerrycans whose handles scraped my fingers and which I courageously carried back to the house and, above all, the flavour that my fatigue gave to the water: it tasted like honey.

The Corpse

'Do you remember your first corpse?'

Uncle Michel talks about my first corpse as if it were my first kiss.

'Yes. I was nine.'

That morning, the *chabeb* (the young fighters) caught a sniper. Anxious to make an example of him, they tied him to the back of a Jeep by his left foot and towed him through the streets of Beirut, honking. Thinking it was a wedding convoy escorting newlyweds, which always proceed amidst a chorus of horns, I stepped out onto the balcony. At first, I must admit, I found the sight of the man being dragged by his foot amusing. But by the third time around, the game began to seem barbaric to me – the sniper's skin had been scraped against the asphalt, and he left a trail of blood in his path.

'*Dakhilkon! Khalsoune!*'

I can still hear his groans, his desperate pleas. He held his hand to his mouth to let the militiamen know that he was thirsty. The Jeep stopped. A sinister-looking man got out. He had a red bandana tied across his forehead. He unscrewed the cap of his canteen and poured a few drops of water between the lips of his prisoner. I was touched by this gesture. But just as the sniper swallowed the liquid, the militiaman, in one swift movement, drew a knife and slit his throat. I saw him brandish the severed head, then put it on the hood of the Jeep. Decked with this trophy, the vehicle started up and resumed its procession through the streets of the capital.

How could anyone forget? Hundreds of kids witnessed it, like me, and had sleepless nights, unable to rid their minds of this image.

'And you, Uncle Michel?'

My uncle shakes his head and puts his hand, yellowed from nicotine, on my shoulder.

'*My* first corpse was my grandfather's. He was lying on a big canopy bed. There were dozens of candles burning around him. He was wearing a black suit, a polka dot tie, and well-polished shoes. My grandmother had powdered his cheeks to give them some colour, and she had done such a good job that upon seeing him I felt as if he were still alive.'

He runs his hand through his white hair, then sighs:

'I said to myself 'I mustn't wake him.' I tiptoed up to him so as not to make any noise, and I kissed his hand. My grandfather was handsome. Even dead he was handsome.'

The Radio

The city is being rebuilt. Yesterday there were tank tracks, today bulldozer tracks. Beirut is a Swiss-cheese city: its buildings, roads and sidewalks are riddled with holes. Its walls bear cracks, like scars.

I park my car and turn towards Françoise, a friend who has just arrived in Lebanon.

'Here is the famous Martyrs' Square,' I tell her, pointing to a deserted esplanade.

The square is not what it used to be. Here, the magnificent Martyrs' Monument once stood imposingly, on a white marble pedestal. Blown to pieces by shell explosions and snipers' bullets, horribly mutilated, the four bronze statues of which it was composed presently lie in wait in a restoration workshop. The most beautiful of them represents a man – or is it a woman? – holding a flame, much like the famous Statue of Liberty. During the war, violent fighting took place here, in the very spot where the statue stood, before the eyes of this creature whose bronze body has long borne stigmata. I miss it – without it, Martyrs' Square is nothing more than an esplanade without a soul.

I start the car back up and drive along the coast. Phoenicia, Saint-Georges, Riviera, Bain Militaire, Raouda, Raouché. The Pigeon Rock stretches across the waves, under the languid stares of soda vendors and Sunday fishermen. There are crowds all along the cliff road: marathon runners wearing headphones; obese walkers; skaters perched on their roller-blades weaving with ballerina-like grace in and out of those strolling along; men eyeing the beautiful women who stream by; idle people killing time … All of Beirut gathers along this seaside avenue every weekend. Workers mix with bankers, women wearing *chadors* with short-skirted nymphets … Differences are blurred, swept away by the sea wind that blows along the cliffs and tousles the palm trees.

'Move along, you slug.'

Stuck in traffic, I am suffocating. The heat is unbearable, the car exhaust and the dust from neighbouring construction sites defile the air.

'Turn on the radio, it'll help you relax,' Françoise advises me.

The radio.

'You know, I haven't touched a radio in seven years.'

'You talk about it as if it were a drug,' she says, smiling.

'During the war, the radio orchestrated our every gesture, our every move, our lives.'

'How so?'

'Radio programs were constantly interrupted by news flashes that advised us to take precautions, to go to the bomb shelters, to not take such-and-such a road ... The messages indicated the precise location of the falling shells; sometimes they even predicted the gunners' next target.'

'And you lived according to the rhythm of the news flashes?'

'We hung on a faceless journalist's every word, dependent upon that bird of ill omen. *Tish tik tish tik* ... The jingle that announced the news flashes terrorized us – it meant that a shell had fallen or was about to fall. It was the harbinger of death.'

Françoise pulls a pack of *Gauloises blondes* cigarettes out of her pocket, takes one out and carefully lights it.

'We didn't have a choice. Can a blind man get by without his cane? In the bomb shelters, at school or at work, people were always listening to the radio; without it, they were completely lost.'

'Did the station have a name?'

'There were at least a dozen stations. Every little group had its frequency, and in the end, this led to a battle of the airwaves that was as violent as the ground battles.'

'A psychological war.'

I shrug my shoulders.

'If you will. A war where there was no room for truth, where all lies were fair play as long as they discredited the adversary.'

Françoise blows out a stream of smoke and says:

'Come on, there are no more shells. Turn on the radio.'

I fiddle with the buttons on my car radio. Majida Roumi's voice resonates:

Aainaka layalén saifiya ...

'What is she saying?' Françoise asks.

'She's saying that "your eyes are like a summer night ..."'

The song is interrupted.

Tish tik tish tik ...

The infamous jingle rings out. Having lost my breath, I slam on the brakes. Françoise goes pale.

'What's happening?' she stammers.

'I don't know,' I say, turning up the volume.

I feel as if I have been catapulted back seven years. I can see myself lying on my bed next to my radio, listening attentively for the latest news from the front, unable to fall asleep.

'*We interrupt this program to announce that ...*'

The journalist's voice is as monotonous as ever and

reveals no hint of emotion; it gives me goosebumps.

> ‘… *Pope Jean-Paul II will visit Lebanon next May. This information has just been confirmed by the Vatican. It will be the Supreme Pontiff's first official visit to the Country of Cedars …*’

I breathe a sigh of relief. Françoise, who didn't understand the announcement – broadcast in Arabic – cannot keep still.

‘Where did they fall?’ she whispers, her eyes bulging.

‘Who?’

‘The shells!’

‘There are no more shells, Françoise. It's the Pope.’

The Candle

War takes us back to the Stone Age. Crouching in the corner of a house – in a corridor, a stairwell – or in a bomb shelter, we forget about comfort, gaining a new appreciation for the simple things in life. Take a candle, for instance. What does a candle mean to a city dweller who lives in London, Paris, Barcelona, Munich, Milan or New York? What purpose can it possibly still serve for such a person? In times of war, a candle is priceless. It is light – the only light that we can hope for when shells force us into hiding, depriving us of power.

This morning at the Notre Dame des Dons church, upon seeing the candles burning on the altar, I became lost in these thoughts. As Beirut was being bombarded by gunfire, such a candle, with a flickering flame, was our sole means of combating the darkness. We learned our lessons by candle-light; played our card games alongside a candle; stole our first kisses after blowing out a candle … When the power was cut in the middle of the night, the same cry would ring out everywhere:

'*Chamaa!*'

'A candle!' Groping around, the youngest among us made his way to the kitchen, blindly opened a drawer and pulled out the precious object.

'And the matches?' he cried out.

'Near the oven.'

He closed the drawer and, eyes opened wide, hands reaching out in front of him, he moved towards the oven.

'Well?' we yelled impatiently.

We heard a crash.

'I broke a plate, but I found the matches,' he said in a reassuring voice.

Then came the crackling of a match. He warmed up the candle to soften the base, pressed it into the middle of a coffee cup and came back, his head held high, brandishing the makeshift lantern that brought light back to us.

When, tired of it all, I would lie down near a candle, I would watch its flame flicker, heeding even the most gentle whispers of the wind. A candle flame is playful: it sways its hips, stretches, contorts itself, a bit like a belly dancer. As it burns down it projects ghostlike shadows on the walls. It exudes tears that slide down its hot body and congeal, just like pearls. As it nears the end, the flame resists with all its might in the midst of its limp, decayed wax body, then silently expires, swallowed up by the newly returned darkness.

The candle is perhaps the most striking example of the incredible generosity of things, and of the ability of certain objects to *love*. It lives and dies for the person for whom it lights the way. Could there be a more beautiful expression of love?

Grenades

'How are the tomatoes looking this year?'

'They're going to be beautiful – you'll see.'

Every time I come across Abou Georges in the vegetable garden, I am reminded of a crazy scene that I witnessed, then took part in, during the war:

One morning, woken with a start by the sound of a gunshot from the garden, I jumped out of bed and, barefoot, ran to find out what was happening. The sight before me rendered me speechless: I saw Abou Georges, pale, brandishing a road sign with a hole in the middle at arm's length and, facing him, Moussa, revolver in hand.

'Moussa! Have you gone mad?'

The taxi driver turned towards me, and with a big smile said:

'It's nothing. Just target practice …'

'Target practice on the gardener? Where do you think you are, the Wild West?'

'It's perfectly safe. I have good aim.'

Moussa had convinced poor Abou Georges to act as his target, and had replaced William Tell's apple with a road sign. Before I had time to reproach him for his act, he dragged me over to his Plymouth. He winked at me, held a finger up to his moustache, and opened the enormous trunk of his car. Strewn around inside were Kalashnikovs, rocket launchers, guns, cartridge belts …

'Take your pick,' he ordered.

'What?'

'Take your pick. I'm offering you the weapon of your choice.'

'Where did you get this arsenal?'

'The militia … Go ahead, pick one.'

'No way.'

Moussa insisted. But he finally gave in to my intransigence.

'At least let me give you a small gift.'

He dug around in the trunk.

'Here,' he finally said, placing an object wrapped in newspaper in the palm of my hand.

He said goodbye to Abou Georges, disappeared into the Plymouth and took off. Intrigued, I felt the package and, without further delay, unwrapped it. My heart stopped – it was a grenade. Up until then, for me, the word '*grenade*'[1] had always referred to the pulpy fruit with red seeds from which Aunt Malaké knew how to extract a sweet syrup. At school I had learned a poem by Paul Valéry:

Dures grenades entr'ouvertes
Cédant à l'excès de vos grains,
Je crois voir des fronts souverains
Éclatés de leurs découvertes!

(Hard pomegranates, split open
Yielding to your overabundance of seeds,
You seem to be sovereign brows
Bursting with their discoveries!)

The *grenade* I had in my hand was different. It

1. 'Grenade' in French also means 'pomegranate'.

resembled a large egg with a rough shell, topped with a pin that made it look like a key chain. I weighed it in my hand – it was much heavier than an egg. With its cast iron, carefully shaped body and its frog-green colour, the grenade reminds us that we must never trust appearances. How can the fact that such a small object can cause so much damage be explained?

Moussa's gift left me feeling perplexed. What was I to do with a grenade in my house? Where could I hide it? I decided to keep it in my dresser, near my bed. But an idea crossed my mind: what would happen if the cleaning woman were to open the drawer too abruptly? Just how sensitive was this grenade?

For two nights, I was unable to fall asleep. The object was a burden to me, I was obsessed with it. Should I throw it out? Yes, but where? How could I throw such a dangerous explosive into the trash? What would happen if the garbage truck were to crush it, or if an alley cat were to inadvertently pull the pin? Who could I turn to for advice? To keep the object was unthinkable, and to get rid of it impossible. I ended up going to Moussa's house. He was taking a nap – I awoke him.

'What? Is the enemy attacking?' he cried out.

'No, no. I just came to return your gift.'

'You don't want it anymore?'

'No,' I replied, putting the grenade in the palm of his hand.

Moussa studied me with a look of dismay. He set the object upright and, frowning, pressed down on a button above the release lever.

'But it's a perfectly good lighter,' he said, watching the little flame that had just shot up.

The Shelter

Eleven o'clock at night. The radio has just announced that bombing has resumed. I leave the house and travel the two hundred yards to the shelter. Along the way, I come across dozens of men in pyjamas and women in nightgowns filing past in the darkness like ghosts. It is a surreal sight, like something out of a dream. The high school principal is dressed in a mauve bathrobe, the priest is wearing flannel long underwear, the baker is in an undershirt, the neighbour has forgotten her wig ... All of these individuals, pulled from their beds by the war, converge around the movie theatre that serves as a bomb shelter. Away from their usual surroundings, without their usual attire, they are hardly recognizable.

Descending the stairway that leads to the ticket booths, I take a quick look at the poster: Sergio Leone's *The Good, the Bad and the Ugly*, starring Clint Eastwood, who is featured on the poster wearing a poncho, squinting, with a cigarillo dangling from the corner of his mouth.

The theatre is huge inside. The neighbourhood's inhabitants push past one another. Each family occupies a small area. This evening the show is not taking place on the screen but outside.

Two hours pass. I need to pee. I open my eyes. For just a second I wonder where I am – I see a dark room, a stage with curtains, and I wonder if I haven't already crossed the border that separates life and death. All around me men, women and children are sitting in the seats sleeping, heads bent forward or leaning back, in an unearthly silence. The explosions, which are shaking the city from above, are hardly audible in here.

The following day, as the guns have not yet been silenced, no one leaves the theatre. To entertain his 'guests', the projectionist shows the advertised film free of charge. His son passes out bags of popcorn. The movie begins in a packed house, piled high with knapsacks and makeshift beds …

> *In this world, my friend, there are two kinds of people: those with loaded guns, and those who dig …*

I am surprised by Clint Eastwood's line. The cowboy is right – there are those who bomb, and those who, either hopeless or fatalistic, dig their graves with their own two hands.

The movie comes to an end amidst applause. I stand up and walk towards the backstage area to stretch my legs. My father has shut himself up in a tiny room that was used as a dressing room for actors when plays used to be put on in the theatre. He is sitting behind a washstand, facing a big mirror. He is writing.

'What are you doing?'

'I'm working … I have some files to finish up.'

'The entire country has been devastated, and you're working!'

'If I stop writing, it will all be over for me.'

I do not persist. I walk through the corridor that connects the artists' dressing rooms. My brothers and sisters are there, wearing wigs and plumed hats, dressed up in embroidered doublets and crinoline dresses they found in the wardrobes.

'Arise, fair sun, and kill the envious moon, who is already sick and pale with grief, that thou her maid art far more fair than she!' one recites, down on one knee.

'I can be forced to live without happiness, but I will never consent to live without honour,' the other replies, sweeping his hand through the air.

I shake my head – they're living in another world. Shells are crashing down on the city, and my brothers and sisters are reciting Shakespeare and Corneille in the dressing rooms of a theatre-turned-bomb shelter.

I continue my tour. Uncle Michel is stretched out on his raincoat. A few steps away from him, a large rat is watching him sleep. I yell out to scare the rodent away. My uncle doesn't even flinch. He is snoring. I feel a lump in my throat. Seventy years old and forced to go to ground like a fox. I recall images of the London Underground during the Second World War that I saw on television – hundreds of old people lying on the bare ground. I clench my fists. How can this still be possible? Where is the international community? According to which criteria does it select the causes that are worth defending? Is it like the stock market? Is there a quotation for the value of human lives? The international community does not exist – it is an abstraction.

A news flash on the radio announces thirty-seven deaths.

In this world, my friend, there are two kinds of people …

Roadblocks

I went back up into the attic of my family home to come to terms with my past. I rediscovered part of my childhood there, thanks to some photographs arranged in a white album: my first bath, my first Christmas, my first communion … I see my uncles and aunts who have passed away, my maternal grandfather and grandmother who died during the war, and these memories tug at my heartstrings. I contemplate a picture of Uncle Jamil, the one who subscribed to *Historia* magazine and who would sing as the shells fell. I am sure that he continues to sing up there. But he must miss *Historia*.

I peruse a series of class pictures. They take me back to my junior high school days, and above all to an experience I thought I had buried. It was an experience that taught me that Death is not a theoretical concept. It is a being made of flesh and blood, whose silhouette can sometimes be seen, whose breath can be felt and whose voice can be heard. During the war, I even shook its hand.

That particular Saturday I had asked Moussa to drive me to Ghada's house. Everything was calm on the front – both sides were counting the previous day's casualties.

'Don't be careless,' he said. 'There's quite a bit of tension along the demarcation line … hostages have been taken.'

'I have to see her, Moussa. At any cost.'

In order to avoid the bridge of death we agreed that it would be best to take the Badaro-Kaskas passageway. I took a seat in the Plymouth and crossed myself:

'It's in God's hands.'

Moussa took out his bottle of Johnnie Walker and took a swig before taking off.

We travelled the first three hundred yards without

a problem. But at an intersection Moussa suddenly stopped and cursed.

'What's going on?'

'There's a moving roadblock,' he stammered. 'We're done for.'

Hooded militiamen had blocked the road with barriers and were checking all vehicles that ventured to take that route.

'What are you afraid of?' I asked Moussa.

'Yesterday evening our guys killed one of their guys at a roadblock. They're probably out for revenge.'

'They can't just take us hostage like that, for no reason.'

The driver glared at me, scowling:

'You don't get it, do you?'

'Anyway, it's too late – we can't turn back now.'

'True,' he admitted, starting the car back up. 'They might fire at us if we do.'

He stopped again at the roadblock. A militiaman armed with a rocket launcher walked up to the Plymouth. He leaned over to inspect the inside of the vehicle, then barked:

'*Aal yamine!*'

'To the right!' meant: 'I don't like the look of you.

Just wait. You'll see what I have in store for you ...' I shuddered. Moussa did not park to the side as the sentry ordered. He rolled down his window and stuck his head out the door to negotiate:

'I'm a taxi driver. I'm doing my job ... And my passenger is a student. For the love of God, let us through.'

The militiaman walked around the car and approached me.

'Roll down your window.'

I obeyed.

'Muslim or Christian?'

He had asked the fateful question, as naturally as Aunt Malaké when she would ask at tea time: 'With sugar or without?'

I did not reply.

'Muslim or Christian?' he repeated, pointing an accusing finger at me.

How was I to respond? It grew silent. I was tempted to lie. But, at the last minute, I got a grip on myself – the passage from the Gospels where Saint Peter denied Christ came back to me ... Also, no sooner would I have lied than I would have been found out – my religion was mentioned on my ID card.

'Christian,' I said in a low voice.

'Get out.'

My heart stopped beating. Moussa panicked. He put his hand on my shoulder and looked at me, aghast. I had no choice – I stepped out of the car. The militiaman signalled to the taxi to turn around and go back, then came towards me:

'I crush little smart-asses like you,' he yelled, pushing me with the butt of his Kalashnikov.

I was penned into a wasteland not far from the roadblock, along with six of my fellow Christians. Our abductors roughed up a woman who was crying; they slapped an old man who was protesting. Paralyzed with fear, I was incapable of intervening. I closed my eyes – my thoughts went out to my parents, and to Ghada. I was angry at myself for not having followed Moussa's advice.

All of a sudden, the man in charge of watching over us took a few steps in my direction. He was wearing a combat uniform in fall colours and a black hood with slits for his eyes, nostrils and mouth. Observing him, I could not help but think of the men in the Ku Klux Klan – like them, this person veiled his face so as to be able to kill unexposed. Did he hope to hide his conscience behind his mask? His eyes, of which I could see only the pupils, were not those of a savage beast, but of a man. How did he end up like this?

He took me by the elbow and pulled me aside. What did he want with me? Were they going to kill the hostages? Why were they starting with me?

'I know you,' the man whispered. 'We were in school together.'

I couldn't help but smile.

'Who are you?'

He held a finger to his lips.

'What are you going to do to us?'

'We have to avenge one of our guys who was killed yesterday at a roadblock like this one.'

'But I had nothing to do with that.'

'You have to pay for the others.'

'Can't you help me?'

My classmate grew silent and thought for a minute.

'Escape through the back,' he finally said. 'I'll say you ran away.'

'Just tell them that we're friends, that we used to play together.'

'They wouldn't understand. To them, a Christian

and a Muslim *cannot* play together.'

'But …'

'Go on, get out of here.'

I squeezed his shoulder.

'Go, run!'

I took to my heels. I ran as fast as I could, without ever looking back. Only today do I finally dare to turn back. What became of the old man who was protesting, and the woman who was moaning? Have they forgiven me for fleeing?

My class pictures are spread out before me. Black and white photographs, yellowed with time. My fingers wander across the shots that look like postcards sent from another country. They are of schoolchildren in grey smocks, smiling at the future … Which of them is the militiaman who pens in hostages in a wasteland? There is no way of knowing – all their faces exude innocence. But I obstinately continue to search – I must find the eyes of the militiaman among the dozens of eyes fixed on the photographer.

I place my index finger on each of my classmates. What has become of them? There are those who have left, those who have stayed.

And the assassins.

Gas

Along the road to the museum, I stop to fill my tank. I park my car at a service station.

'Five gallons!'

The attendant is Egyptian. He is wearing orange coveralls that make him look like an astronaut. He hurries over, clears the pump, lifts the hatch to my gas tank, unscrews my gas cap, then inserts the adjustable-flow nozzle into the tank. The metre very quickly reads '5'. The Egyptian shuts off the pump. I pay, get back into my car and take off.

'Amazing,' I say to myself, looking at my watch.

'Three minutes for five gallons of gas.'

The last time, during the war, the process had taken *eight* hours. At that time, due to the shipping blockade, the country was experiencing an unprecedented gas shortage. To get around and to his office my father would while away the hours in the endless queues that formed at the service stations. In the oppressive heat – many drivers stripped right down to their undershirts – he would wait his turn, his hands folded together on top of the steering wheel. To avoid being short of gas he often stocked cans of it on the kitchen balcony, much to the dismay of my mother, who was afraid that the slightest spark would set off a catastrophe. To fill the tank of his car with the stocked gas, my father had two techniques: the funnel and the rubber hose. For the funnel, he would ask me to hold the object firmly in place above the gas tank while he poured his precious yellowish liquid into it; for the hose, he would stick one end of it in the can, take the other end in his mouth, suck forcefully to pump out the gas, then plunge that end into the tank; as if by magic, the gas would be decanted. Some days the crisis reached alarming proportions. Thieves would scour parking lots, breaking open gas tanks and, thanks to the rubber hose technique, extracting the gas of others.

One morning, my eldest brother, who prided himself on being good in chemistry, advised us in order to save gas to add water and mothballs to it, one pound of mothballs to one litre of water. The result was immediate and acute: our father's car spent two weeks at the mechanic's!

We discovered the virtues of walking and biking. Tyres that go flat, chains that fall off, painful falls in streams … none of these discouraged us. As for Uncle Michel, he bought a donkey. He tied it up in the back courtyard and did not hesitate to use it to get around town. 'You'll see,' he would say. 'Soon everyone will be copying me.' Giving in to my requests, he allowed me to accompany him. He sat me down behind him and advised me to put my arms around him and hold on very tight so as not to fall off. Responding to his signal, the donkey set off, twitching its ears. The ride was pleasant – lulled by the sound of hooves on the road, I sat up above the cars around us and enjoyed an incomparable view over the city. As we turned the corner, we found ourselves in front of a service station that was swarming with people – three queues, each a hundred yards long, converged on the pump. Having run out of patience, the motorists were gesticulating, yelling, swearing. The attendant was doing his best to ward off the onslaught.

'Hey! There's Uncle Michel with his donkey!'

Forgetting their quarrels, the drivers turned towards us. Some began to yell out loud hee-haws, others burst out laughing, pointing at us. My uncle did not flinch. He continued on his way, chest out, head held high, noble and proud like a desert *emir* on his steed.

'Ignore them.' he said to me in a low voice. 'They don't know what the time they're wasting is worth …'

One Shell All

'Tonight's football game is between Liverpool and Manchester United. Both teams are on their way out of the locker rooms now, preceded by the referee …'

Football has always been my passion. Moreover, during the war, it was the passion of an entire people. How could I not think of that time while watching this game? The year is 1982. Spain is hosting the World Cup. Lebanon is being set ablaze, battles raging on every front; the population is fired up about the teams in the competition. Strangely, the country's loyalties are divided: on one side are those rooting for the German team, the symbol of rigour and discipline; on the other, those rooting for Brazil, the symbol of virtuosity and extravagance. I remember my neighbourhood on the eve of the 1982 World Cup kick-off: the streets drowning under a flood of green and gold – or black, red and yellow banners; apartment buildings decked in flags; on the walls, graffiti glorifying both teams; on car windshields, portraits of the players … It was during the opening game that I came to understand the extent to which the belligerent groups took an interest in sports – not a single shot was fired during the entire Argentina-Belgium game. For a full hour and a half the heart of the war stopped beating. The guns held their breath. On the radio, news flashes ceased to list the names of casualties. The same phenomenon occurred the following day, then throughout the competition, as if the war suddenly fell in tune with the sport. Before and after the game, the shells fell at a dizzying rate; during the game, peace and quiet reigned. It was an unbearable ritual: a reprieve from death and the illusion of peace within the space of two half-times. The intensity of the fighting to come often depended on the outcome of a game – the west side of the capital was rooting for Brazil, and the east side for Germany, and when one of the two teams emerged victorious the fighters supporting it would display their elation by bombing the enemy camp.

Hidden away in the bomb shelters, their eyes riveted on little television sets that, due to a lack of electricity, were plugged into car batteries, the population forgot everything and became worked up upon seeing the twenty-two players fighting over a ball. Even women got caught up in the excitement, urging on the men wiggling their hips in their shorts on the football pitch, insulting the referee or giving free reign to their euphoria. When the final whistle blew, before the artillery battles resumed, some fans, unable to restrain themselves any longer, would go out into the streets to express their satisfaction at having won or would drive back and forth through the neighbourhood in their cars, their hands glued to their horns. Sometimes scuffles would break out, which would come to an end when the fighting resumed.

The referee's whistle signalling the kick-off for the Liverpool-Manchester United game tears me away from my memories. How many human lives were spared during those rare moments when the guns were silenced? How many deaths avoided thanks to Brian Robson and his team-mates?

Alcohol

The clock in the living room chimes six times. I settle in on the terrace, a bottle of arrack in hand. The sun is sinking below the horizon. It is bathed in a pool of light, a bit like Monsieur Jabbour, Uncle Michel's childhood friend, who was found in the middle of the road, bathed in a pool of blood, a hole between his eyes. He was wearing a blue shirt, the colour of tonight's sky which is turning red. 'There is something immodest about watching a sunset,' Uncle Michel used to say. 'It should be allowed to die in peace.' Try as I might to assure him that it was OK because it would be back the next day, there was no convincing him – he would twist his face into a grimace. He would scratch his forehead, then declare in a solemn voice: 'You have to be naive to believe that the sun that disappears is the same one that will return tomorrow – every passing day sees the death of a sun.'

Françoise joins me.

'Is that anisette?' she asks, pointing with her chin towards the bulbous bottle I am expertly caressing.

'It's pretty close.'

I pour the clear liqueur into a small glass. I add a little bit of water to it. The glass turns a milky white.

'That reminds me of experiments in chemistry class.'

'Chemistry is exactly what it is – arrack converts dreariness into delight.'

I lift the glass to my nose and breathe in deeply.

'Ah, the smell of arrack. It goes straight to your head, cleanses your mind. During the war, we were all arrack drinkers.'

'In order to forget?'

I take small sips of my drink and click my tongue against my palate each time I swallow.

'To forget, yes. Sometimes, when shells were falling

on our neighbourhood and everyone was taking refuge in the bomb shelters, I would swill down an entire bottle of arrack. I would go out onto the balcony, throw out my arms and sing.'

'You were crazy, my friend,' Françoise murmurs, tapping her forehead with her index finger.

'Alcohol *denies* danger. I wasn't even aware of the risks I was taking by exposing myself to the bombs. I wasn't thinking of anything. I was euphoric, carefree, lighthearted.'

'It could have cost you your life!'

'My mother would beg me to come back inside, would pull me by my shirt tails … But it was no use – I was too engrossed in the show.'

Françoise scowls:

'What show?'

'The rockets cutting across the sky! They looked like shooting stars, like comets. I would follow their trajectory with my finger, the golden furrows they traced, the showers of sparks that flew through the darkness and lit up part of my city. I would sing out, loud and clear, off-key, accompanying the symphony of lights.'

Françoise can't believe it. She tosses her hair back, and in a solemn voice says:

'Waking up must have been awful.'

'In the morning I was back to square one. I would wake up with a hangover. Everyone would tell me: 'You sang all night.' And as for me, I couldn't remember anything.'

I drink my fifth glass of arrack. My ears get hot. The terrace is reeling. The plants and the furniture come loose. Françoise is floating through the air. I am sinking. I grab onto her dress. She laughs.

Drunkards are forgiven everything, for they know not what they do.

The Long Vacation

I open the door to the café in Gemmayzé, one of Beirut's oldest neighbourhoods. I sit down at a table and look around me and I see nothing but old men with grey hair, their collars open, spending their time whiling it away. They are either playing backgammon or cards. The waiter goes from table to table proposing *narghiles*. Every day it's the same ritual – they are sinking ships. Some are widowers or are divorced, others what we call 'confirmed bachelors'. All have as a home base this café oddly dubbed '*Qahwat el-Azaz*' (The Glass Café), maybe because its façade is a glass wall that looks out onto the street. As you step into this tobacco-infested place it immediately becomes clear that you are disturbing these people: dozens of near-sighted eyes turn towards you, and look you over from head to toe. The ambience has not changed in ages – the café's regulars have a few more wrinkles, that is all.

For years we were just like these men – we spent our time whiling it away. Drowning our anxiety in games. Doing what we could so the hours would pass without our noticing, under the illusion that we would find peace at the end of a game. Before the war I knew nothing about cards – I held them fanned out in such a disorganized manner that I gave my hand away every time. By the end of the war no game remained that had not revealed its secrets to me. By candlelight, we spent our quiet evenings – which they all were – in the company of the king, queen and jack. Some took up chess, others preferred backgammon. As for my mother and my aunts, they endlessly knitted hats, sweaters and mittens, so much so that they had a terrible time unloading the products of their industry.

Mornings were devoted to strolling in the countryside. The area where we had taken refuge was one of the most diverse in the Kesruan region. It offered a wide variety of trees, plants and insects that brought us happiness during the long vacation granted to us by the war. I spent hours in the fields gathering thyme – an essential ingredient for the preparation of *manakich*, a sort of breakfast pie – or lavender that Aunt Malaké put into little sachets to be used for perfuming closets. Thanks to my mother, I learned to call plants by their names: *Rhododendron ponticum* with its flowering clusters, *Erica verticillata*, more commonly known as 'heather', *Convolvulus arvensis*, the code name for bindweed, *Ixiolirion tataricum*, alias Siberian lily …

When it was nice out I picnicked with my brothers and sisters in the shade of the oak trees; I slept beneath the willow trees near the springs and the rivulets; I helped pick olives, pine cones and apples. My father worried, seeing me lying on my stomach observing ants and lizards. But my mother set his mind at rest: 'It's science,' she said. 'That's how Konrad Lorenz got his start.' As for my older brother, he chased flies and bees, and stalked through the yard armed with his plastic fly swatter. Every evening he diligently wrote down the results of his day's work in a notebook: 'thirty flies downed, seventeen bees squished', a little bit like pilots who mark an X on their fuselage for every plane they shoot down. Occasionally he indulged in amazing experiments: he put a grasshopper and a spider together in a transparent box and devoted three hours of his time to observing the two insects' reactions ... There were also mosquitoes and butterflies which, at nightfall, came and hovered around our candles. We did not chase them away – they livened up our nights, much like the frogs and cicadas that lulled us with their croaking and chirping.

It was at that time that *Le Petit Baigneur* (*The Little Bather*) came into being. It was an apolitical weekly magazine of which I was the founder and the sole contributing writer, and whose name was a reference to a film starring Louis de Funès. Only one copy was released each week, presented in the form of a thirty-page notebook, entirely handwritten. I rented it out to my brothers, sisters, cousins and friends for the modest sum of fifty piastres. With the gold mine I pulled in by doing this I bought prizes for the lucky winners of my magazine's contests.

Uncle Michel helped us occupy our spare time. He put on plays in the yard. Thus, under his direction, we acted out the Rahbani Brothers' *Petra*, as well as

Schéhadé's *The Emigrant of Brisbane* and Giraudoux's *Tiger at the Gates*, which were a big hit among our parents and neighbours. To get us to stretch our legs he organized some special Olympic Games with categories we could handle – track and cycling. The opening day of the Games we paraded past the audience wearing tracksuits and brandishing flags. At the close of the competition winners and losers alike were awarded chocolate medals, which they received atop a makeshift podium, to the sound of the national anthem.

'*Chéch béch!*'

Seeing the café's regulars blow into their fists and expertly roll the dice, I could not help but think about the best part of the war – if there can be anything good about a war, that is: those idle moments that it granted us, thanks to which we were reconciled with nature and with time.

The Hospital

It hedge-hops, circles around the flame, rises up into the air, then does a nosedive. Its wings catch fire. We hear them sizzle. The moth goes into a tailspin and lands at the base of the candle. Another, smaller one suddenly springs forth out of the darkness. It draws near my youngest brother and encircles him. Irritated, my brother swats at it with the back of his hand. Flustered, the moth takes refuge in the hollow of his ear.

'Mom!'

My brother jumps up out of his seat, panicking.

'The moth! It flew into my ear!'

He starts to cry. Stuck to his eardrum, the moth flutters. My mother is worried.

'I've never heard of anything like this happening before.' she says, shrugging her shoulders.

She looks into his ear, tries to dislodge the moth with a Q-tip. Nothing works.

'To the hospital!'

She takes my brother by the hand, pushes him into the car and heads for the nearest hospital. After a minute she jumps with a start:

'What are you doing here?'

She had not seen me.

'I'm coming with you, Mom.'

'No one asked you to come,' she curtly replies.

Five minutes later we arrive at the emergency room. My mother goes up to a nurse:

'Excuse me, Miss, it's my son – he has a …'

She does not finish her sentence. With a violent kick, a bearded militiaman has just opened the door. Followed by half a dozen armed fighters, he shoves past everyone and barges into the operating room.

'Who's in charge here?' he barks.

A doctor rushes over, trembling.

'Treat him!' the bearded man orders, pointing

towards the militiaman lying on a stretcher.

The doctor leans over the inert body. He lifts the eyelids, runs his stethoscope over his hairy chest.

'There's nothing more we can do,' he says in an almost inaudible voice.

'What did you say?' the bearded man mutters, raising his index finger.

'He's ... untreatable.'

The militiaman flies into a rage, gesticulating and swearing at the doctor, the hospital and all of Hippocrates' s disciples. Losing patience, he draws his gun and points it at the doctor's temple. His protruding eyes are bloodshot.

'You have fifteen minutes to save him. Or else ...'

I whisper into Mom's ear:

'Or else what?'

'Be quiet, you idiot,' she whispers, pinching me.

The doctor knows that he cannot save the dead man. But he wants to save his own neck. He bluffs to gain some time, hoping the militiamen will eventually calm down.

'Follow me!'

The nurses set the corpse on a gurney and follow along behind him. The militiamen clear out of the operating room. Fifteen minutes later, the doctor comes out, conspicuously raising his gloved, blood-stained hands up in the air to show that he has done all that was medically possible.

'It's over,' he murmurs.

The militiamen break down. The bearded man approaches the doctor and embraces him. Leaning his forehead on his shoulder, he blubbers like a child.

Outside, it is raining shells. Ambulance sirens are screeching. Standing up against the wall of the corridor, we hold our breath. Dozens of wounded, limbs twisted, covered with blood, file past us. My mother puts her hand over my youngest brother's eyes.

'Don't look!' she orders, as if it were a risqué scene on television.

A fetid odour of alcohol, formol and excrement infests the air. The nurses push back the new arrivals – the hospital is full. That is what war is: these wounded who have lost an eye, a leg, an arm, who cry out every time they breathe; these men and women who are transported to the morgue in garbage bags.

'Can I help you?'

The doctor has stopped and is looking at my mother with inquiring eyes. She relaxes her lips, but no sound comes out of her mouth. Her little one's case is so derisory compared to all of these horrors.

'I have a moth in my left ear,' my brother replies.

The doctor frowns. My mother pinches my brother and stammers:

'Nothing serious, doctor. We'll come back another day.'

Refugees

'Come, come quick. A policeman is trying to evict Abou Georges and his family!'

I push back my chair, leave the dining room and run to find out what is happening. In the basement of the neighbouring apartment building, there is a huge commotion. A police officer is there, in his grey uniform and cap with a silver cedar emblem. Abou Georges is gesticulating, shouting angrily, yelling threats. In a corner, his wife and two children are crying.

'They're trying the old '*Allah Maak*' on me again,' he

says to me, trembling with rage. 'This time I won't let them get away with it!'

'*Allah Maak!*'

One day, the police showed up at Abou George's house and said to him: '*Allah Maak!*': 'May God be with you.' Abou Georges did not immediately understand the meaning of these two words. But when the militiamen pressed the barrel of a gun against his temple he understood. His wife and kids packed their bags – two small suitcases in which they arranged the bare essentials. The following day, at dawn, they left their village in the Chouf region on a tractor. Along the exile route there was an endless procession: hundreds of uprooted families in pyjamas or tracksuits; cars crammed full; adolescents carrying old people on their backs or in wheelbarrows … Abou Georges held his head in his hands. To boost his spirits a Red Cross worker assured him that the UN was going to get involved, that all those who had been displaced would return home within a week's time.

Abou Georges ended up near our house, in the basement of an apartment building, among other refugees. At first, time seemed to pass slowly. He grew impatient, unable to conceive that the UN could be so slow to react. Gradually he came to understand that the return he hoped for was not to take place in the near future. One morning he was informed that the militia had blown up his house: 'Not a stone was left standing,' he was told. The shock was so great that he passed out.

Without a word to his family, Abou Georges began to go through the trash. He found chunks of bread that he secretly heated up and gave to his children. 'I dream that I've gone home, that I'm sleeping in *my* bed, in *my* house,' he confided to me one day. 'But when I wake up, I realize that reality is different: I'm sleeping in a parking lot, among cars. I have been deprived of my house. I have been forcefully exiled in my own country. I have lost everything. Even hope.' I proposed that he do the gardening at my parents' house. He accepted without the slightest hesitation.

'*Allah Maak!*' the policeman repeats.

I intervene.

'On what grounds are you evicting him?'

'Squatting in parking lots is prohibited.'

He hands me the order from the Court of Beirut. I quickly read over it. I linger over the last lines: 'We order the eviction of Mr Abou Georges and his family.'

'Read, read the first line,' yells Abou Georges.

'*Bismmel chaab al loubnani*': 'In the name of the Lebanese people.'

The gardener forces out a laugh.

'Ha! "In the name of the Lebanese people." If that is the will of the Lebanese people, to turn its refugees out into the streets, well shame on the Lebanese people.'

'Calm down, Abou Georges. Show them your refugee card.'

He disappears for a minute, then comes back triumphantly brandishing a laminated card that he hands to the police officer.

'I am an official refugee. Look, it's written here, in black and white.'

The policeman hardly glances at it, shrugs his shoulders.

'These cards are no longer valid. They expired ...'

Abou Georges is crestfallen. He throws himself in my arms and sobs. His hair smells like damp earth.

'I'm sick of this,' he stammers. 'I'm going to leave this crappy country ...'

'Where will you go?'

'To Sweden. I hear that they treat political refugees well there.'

'But you can't request political asylum. You aren't being persecuted.'

Abou Georges shakes his head:

'We've been persecuted for fifteen years.'

Car Bombs

'Happy Mother's Day, Mom!'

In Lebanon, Mother's Day falls on the first day of spring. This is not a coincidence. I place a kiss on my mother's forehead.

'You are my sunshine,' she says, squeezing my hands.

She takes the bouquet of roses that I hand her and walks towards the dining room. Sitting in the corner of the living room, I observe her. I know her every move by heart. My mother … I am always afraid of losing her, of no longer being able to see her eyes. During the war, I was constantly watching her, protecting her, not only out of love and devotion, but also because my own equilibrium depended on hers. One May morning – how could I forget? – my mother left the house to do some shopping at a supermarket that was three hundred yards from our house. I had my nose in my books; I replied to her farewell with a nod of my head.

A half-an-hour later, an extremely violent explosion shook the entire city. The windows of our house shattered. I threw myself flat on the ground, my hands clasped behind my neck.

'What was that?' my father asked, getting back up.

We looked at him, dazed, unsure where the explosion had originated. Taking his courage in both hands, my youngest brother went to find out what had happened. He returned shortly after and told us, his voice tight with emotion:

'A car bomb … Apparently it exploded near the supermarket.'

'Mom!' Without thinking, I rushed out of the house. In the distance wreaths of smoke swirled in the sky. I raced the three hundred yards to the location of the explosion. 'God, let her have changed her mind at the last minute … Let her not have been hurt … Let her still be alive …' Out of breath, completely distraught, I arrived in front of the supermarket. The sight before my eyes petrified me: a thick, black cloud of smoke had swooped down on the area; here and there, there were charred, overturned vehicles; everywhere traces of blood, scraps of flesh, fragments of glass, rubble … Ambulance drivers and firemen scattered in every direction. Cries, groans mingled with screeching sirens. I approached a rescue worker:

'My mother is in there!'

'Get away from here!'

'How many casualties?'

'One-hundred-and-thirty-six.'

'A car bomb?'

'A Peugeot set to explode during a peak shopping period …'

'*Please*, make sure my mother is safe and sound.'

The worker took down my mother's name and went to check with the ambulance drivers to see if she was on the list of casualties. The few minutes that I had to wait for the 'verdict' dragged on forever. So, my mother's life depended on chance, on a name on a list. The entire war is the very image of this tragedy: a vile lottery. After this episode, how could I not live in fear?

And how could I bear a grudge against those who, terrorized by these infernal machines, refuse to return to this country?

'She isn't on the list.'

The rescue worker's response was like a deliverance.

'Thank you God, thank you!'

I headed home, at a slow pace.

On the steps of my family home stood my mother, her hands on her hips:

'Where were you, you thoughtless fool?' she yelled indignantly. 'You scared me to death.'

The Schoolteacher

I feel compelled to visit my old elementary school. I walk into the classroom as I would a cathedral. I sit down in my seat, the third row next to the window. I open the desk – my name is still there, carved into the wood. I fold my hands and look straight ahead. I hear the teacher calling on me:

'Go to the board!'

I slap my hand to my chest.

'Me?'

'Yes, you!'

I grudgingly stand up.

'Go on, "Cazeneuve".'

I have borne this nickname for quite some time. My classmates call me this because I got a good grade on the commentary of a text by Jean Cazeneuve about television.

I step up onto the platform, my hands behind my back. I am weak at the knees.

'Please recite Prévert's "Histoire du cheval" ("Tale of the Horse").'

I swallow, take a deep breath like a swimmer getting ready to dive and begin the declamation:

Braves gens écoutez ma complainte
Écoutez l'histoire de ma vie

(Good people hear my lament
Hear the story of my life)

A shell explodes. The windows shake. I stop.

'Go on,' the teacher says. 'Don't let it intimidate you.'

Et comme il y avait la guerre
la guerre qui continuait
la vie devenait chère
les vivres diminuaient

(And as there was the war
the war that carried on
life was becoming dear
provisions were growing scarce)

The bombing intensifies. The teacher is worried, I can tell. My classmates fidget on their benches. Their whispers travel to where I am standing. I raise my voice to make myself heard.

Maintenant la guerre est finie
et le vieux général est mort
est mort dans son lit
mort de sa belle mort
mais moi je suis …

(Now the war is over
and the old general has died
died in his sleep
died a peaceful death
but I am …)

A shell has just landed on the roof of the school. The blast of the explosion nearly knocks me over. But I am experienced. A supervisor is running through the halls yelling: 'To the shelters!' The bell rings before the end of the hour. The teacher picks up his briefcase.

'I'll call on you another time,' he says, getting up.

'Please, sir, let me finish.'

I have reached the end of my poem. I do not want to start all over again.

Mais moi je suis vivant et c'est le principal
bonsoir
bonne nuit
bon appétit mon général.

(But I am alive and that is what matters above all
good evening
good night
sleep tight General.)

* * *

I found my teacher in Paris where he had gone into exile. He still teaches French, but he has removed 'Histoire du cheval' from his syllabus. It must bring back painful memories. He invited me for a drink at his place. I avoided talking about school. He played

Jacques Brel and Barbara for me. He served me some red wine. And then, unable to resist any longer, he went and got a stack of papers out of a drawer.

'Read these, Cazeneuve.'

I smiled – he remembered. I took the papers and leafed through them.

'These are essays …'

'Yes. I brought a few with me.'

'What's so special about them?'

'Read them!'

I picked one out at random. Subject: 'What does it mean to like to take risks?'

> *Along the path to my house there is a sniper. Every day, after school, I go out on the balcony and thumb my nose at him. That is what it means to like to take risks.*

I picked out another paper. 'A Serge Lama song, entitled "*Souvenirs, attention danger*" ("Memories, beware of danger"). What does this title mean to you?'

> *We found my father in the trunk of a car. I was there.*

He had not had anything stolen. He had been killed because of his religion. I cannot think about this memory any more. Otherwise there will be danger.

My teacher took his head in his hands. I pulled another from the stack: 'Describe your house.'

My house was pretty. It had a view of the Mediterranean. One day, the militia from both camps came and they occupied my house. Not at the same time – they took turns. In my room, some of them wrote slogans praising their leader. In the living room, the others ripped up his portrait and spit on it.

I continued: 'What is the verse that you appreciate most, and why?'

'A verse by Elia Abu-Madi:

'Pays des étoiles, je suis là.
Regarde bien: ne me reconnais-tu pas?'

(Land of stars, I am here.
Look closely – don't you recognize me?)

I am moved by this poem because we have become strangers in our own country.

Subject: 'You borrow a time machine. Imagine what you would do.'

If I had a time machine, I would go back to the time of Creation. I would go ask God: Why?

I put the stack of papers back in its place.

'They were twelve- and thirteen-year-olds,' my teacher said. Normally, at that age, kids dream.'

Epilogue

On the white tablecloth, next to a large basket filled with tomatoes, cucumbers and lettuce, the waiter has set out the *mezze*: there is *mtabal* garnished with parsley and cumin, *tabouli*, stuffed grape leaves, a dish of *hummus*, a plate of *falafel* ... All the members of my family are seated around the table, including Uncle Michel and Aunt Malaké. Uncle Michel clears his throat and offers a word of welcome, lifting his glass of arrack to 'the one who came back.' Tears come to my eyes. To exorcize the war, I fled. But in fleeing I nearly forgot my family, all those who are gathered around this table, dipping their bread into the same dish as I.

'If Big Bertha comes back will you leave again?' my uncle asks.

I protest: 'You know very well that I didn't leave until the end of the war. I wasn't afraid of your Big Bertha.'

'True. But would you have the strength to relive what you experienced?'

I think for a moment, then reply. 'What I experienced I relive every day, in spite of myself – one doesn't come through a war unscathed.'

'Why come back when most of your friends are leaving, disappointed?' Aunt Malaké asks.

'Disappointed by what?'

'By the economic crisis, the scars of the war, the chaos …'

'Aunt Malaké, I am among those who believe that it is our duty to assume our destiny in the country where we were born.'

I pour myself some arrack. Uncle Michel launches into an endless speech – his wartime memories, like an old veteran. In his remarks, there is no room for blood, suffering or casualties. He speaks of the dull roar of the cannonade, the courage of the population which, early in the morning, rebuilt what the shells had destroyed the previous day, his lack of concern in the face of hails of bullets, his donkey, the long card games played by candlelight …

'Tell me, Uncle Michel, you wouldn't be in love with Big Bertha, would you?'

Uncle Michel jumps. He turns towards me and winks:

'You want to know the truth? Big Bertha is a bitch!'